DOGS WITH JOBS

Guard Dogs

Rochelle Groskreutz
and Katie Gillespie

MEDIA ENHANCED BOOKS AV2 BY WEIGL ADDED VALUE • AUDIO VISUAL
www.av2books.com

AV² provides enriched content that supplements and complements this book. Weigl's AV² books strive to create inspired learning and engage young minds in a total learning experience.

Your AV² Media Enhanced books come alive with...

Audio
Listen to sections of the book read aloud.

Key Words
Study vocabulary, and complete a matching word activity.

Video
Watch informative video clips.

Quizzes
Test your knowledge.

Embedded Weblinks
Gain additional information for research.

Slide Show
View images and captions, and prepare a presentation.

Try This!
Complete activities and hands-on experiments.

... and much, much more!

Go to www.av2books.com, and enter this book's unique code.

BOOK CODE

AVM78537

AV² by Weigl brings you media enhanced books that support active learning.

Published by AV² by Weigl
350 5th Avenue, 59th Floor
New York, NY 10118
Website: www.av2books.com

Library of Congress Cataloging-in-Publication Data
Names: Groskreutz, Rochelle, author. | Gillespie, Katie, author.
Title: Guard dogs / Rochelle Groskreutz and Katie Gillespie.
Description: New York, NY : AV2 by Weigl, [2020] | Series: Dogs with jobs | Audience: Grade 4 to 6. | Includes index.
Identifiers: LCCN 2018053404 (print) | LCCN 2018054176 (ebook) | ISBN 9781489699084 (Multi User Ebook) | ISBN 9781489699091 (Single User Ebook) | ISBN 9781489699060 (hardcover : alk. paper) | ISBN 9781489699077 (softcover : alk. paper)
Subjects: LCSH: Watchdogs--Juvenile literature.
Classification: LCC SF428.8 (ebook) | LCC SF428.8 .G76 2020 (print) | DDC 636.73--dc23
LC record available at https://lccn.loc.gov/2018053404

Printed in Guangzhou, China
1 2 3 4 5 6 7 8 9 0 23 22 21 20 19

012019
103118

Editor: Katie Gillespie Art Director: Terry Paulhus

Weigl acknowledges Getty Images, Alamy, and iStock as its primary image suppliers for this title. Every reasonable effort has been made to trace ownership and to obtain permission to reprint copyright material. The publishers would be pleased to have any errors or omissions brought to their attention so that they may be corrected in subsequent printings.

CONTENTS

Guarding What Matters

Have you ever gone past a fenced yard and had a dog run towards you? Was that dog barking, growling, or showing its sharp teeth? If so, you may have met a guard dog.

Guard dogs have an important job. They keep people, property, and other animals safe.

There are three main kinds of guard dogs. **Security** guard dogs work for businesses. **Livestock** guard dogs work on farms. Personal guard dogs work for families.

German pinschers were originally bred to catch rats. Today, these intelligent dogs can be trained for all kinds of different jobs, including guarding.

Doberman pinschers are known for their guarding ability and fearlessness. These loyal dogs develop close relationships with their owners.

Safely by Your Side

Dogs have lived side by side with people for about 32,000 years. They were the first animals that ancient humans **tamed** as pets. These dogs helped their owners hunt, guarded their families, and were faithful friends.

The guard dogs that worked in ancient times watched over castles, people, and precious objects such as gold. In ancient Rome, dogs watched over property. One of Rome's great poets, Virgil, talked about his guard dogs in his poem *Georgics*. Published in the year 29 BC, the poem claims that, "Never, with them on guard, need you fear for your stall a midnight thief…"

A Big, Brave Job

A guard dog's job is dangerous. Security guard dogs that work for businesses can bark and attack **intruders** to scare them away. These dogs are trained to act alone.

Livestock guard dogs that protect farm animals are also at risk. If not trained properly, these dogs can be bitten or even killed by **predators** such as coyotes.

Personal guard dogs can bark and attack too, but only on command from their owners. They are trained to be friendly to their family members, but not to take commands from strangers. They could also be poisoned or be hurt by strangers.

A Life of Work as Play

The lives of skilled guard dogs are all about training, performing, and doing their best. Security guard dogs are trained for specific tasks. They might search rooms and buildings, or protect objects and areas.

Guard dogs work for about 7 to 10 years. On and off duty, these dogs live with their **handlers**. They follow their handlers' every command.

FACTS UNLEASHED

Personal guard dogs spend their days protecting people and property. They are a loyal, loving part of a family, and are gentle around children.

Trained to Protect

Guard dogs can start training when they are as young as six months old. They first master basic **obedience**, following only their handler's simple words or hand signal commands. These dogs are trained to bark at strangers, yet not to be distracted by what is around them.

Some guard dogs go through hours of testing with special trainers to make sure they are comfortable in many different situations. They might need to climb narrow stairs, move on slippery floors, or be around many loud noises.

Guard dogs can be trained to attack. Trainers wear a glove and tap the dog's face to bother the dog. They shout "attack" until the dog understands the command. Trainers may also use human-sized dolls as intruders. The dogs are taught to attack these dolls on command.

Livestock guard dogs are trained to bark warnings. They attack by charging dangerous animals or pinning them down if they threaten the herd. These dogs also learn to be comfortable doing their job among a crowded herd of animals.

Training time can vary, depending on the guard dog's job. Some dogs can be trained in as little as four weeks. However, it takes at least a year to properly train most guard dogs.

FACTS UNLEASHED

Livestock guard dogs grow up with the animals they protect. This helps them feel like one of the herd, so they protect it better. These dogs work long hours and live with the herd as much as possible.

Guard Dog Hero: Odin

On October 8, 2017, outside his farmstead in Northern California, Roland Hendel smelled smoke. The bright orange sky warned him of the nearby Tubbs Wildfires. Minutes later, he and his daughter Ariel drove away, barely escaping the rolling flames behind them. Odin, his faithful Great Pyrenees livestock guard dog, stayed behind.

Mr. Hendel could not separate Odin from his flock of goats. Odin was even willing to separate from his sister, Tessa. The two dogs had never spent more than a day apart since Mr. Hendel had adopted them as puppies to help care for his goats. Mr. Hendel had rescued the goats, too, and had built them a barn.

Two days later, Mr. Hendel and Ariel returned to find everything ruined, with trees burning around them. They feared the worst for Odin and the goats. Then, they spotted furry patches running in the distance.

Goats raced towards them, unharmed except for one who had a small burn. Following close behind was a hobbling dog with singed fur and melted whiskers. It was Odin! Not only had the brave dog saved the goats, several baby deer were also huddled around him for safety. All of the animals recovered, and Odin is still guarding his goats today.

Meeting Guard Dogs

Since guard dogs are not friendly to strangers, never touch them unless their owner is there and gives you permission. Back away slowly from a guard dog that is growling or showing its teeth. Running away can cause it to chase or attack you.

FACTS UNLEASHED

What is the difference between a watchdog and a guard dog? Watchdogs are trained to bark to warn of intruders. Guard dogs are trained to bark and also attack intruders, if needed.

What Makes a Good Guard Dog?

Not every breed of dog makes an ideal guard dog. Successful guard dogs must be strong, be able to listen well and think fast, and have lots of energy. Doberman pinschers, German shepherds, Great Pyrenees, rottweilers, and mastiffs are some of the breeds that make good guard dogs.

When picking the right guard dog for the job, female dogs are usually better at protecting people because of their **maternal** nature. Male dogs are often better at watching over property. It is in their nature to guard their **territory**.

FACTS UNLEASHED

The biggest, heaviest guard dog is the English mastiff. It can weigh as much as a washing machine!

Quiz

1 What kind of animals did Odin protect?

2 Who was the Roman poet who wrote about his guard dogs in the year 29 BC?

3 The livestock guard dog Odin saved his flock from what?

4 What are the three main kinds of guard dogs?

5 At what age can guard dogs start their training?

6 What kind of guard dog lives on a farm?

7 Are male or female guard dogs usually better at protecting property?

8 How long have dogs lived side by side with people?

9 What should you do if a guard dog growls at you or shows you its teeth?

10 What breed of guard dog can weigh as much as a washing machine?

ANSWERS

1 Goats **2** Virgil **3** Fire **4** Security guard dogs, livestock guard dogs, and personal guard dogs **5** Six months **6** Livestock guard dog **7** Male dogs **8** About 32,000 years **9** Back away slowly **10** English mastiff

Key Words

handlers: people who live and work with security guard dogs

intruders: people who go somewhere without being welcome, usually to commit a crime

livestock: animals kept or raised on a farm, usually to be sold

maternal: feelings or actions typical of a mother

obedience: an act of following a command

predators: animals that prey on other animals

security: freedom from danger

tamed: domesticated; made less dangerous or powerful

territory: an area of land that an animal guards

Index

Log on to www.av2books.com

AV² by Weigl brings you media enhanced books that support active learning. Go to www.av2books.com, and enter the special code found on page 2 of this book. You will gain access to enriched and enhanced content that supplements and complements this book. Content includes video, audio, weblinks, quizzes, a slide show, and activities.

AV² Online Navigation

Audio
Listen to sections of the book read aloud.

Book Pages
AV² pages directly correspond to pages in the book.

Video
Watch informative video clips.

Embedded Weblinks
Gain additional information for research.

Key Words
Study vocabulary, and complete a matching word activity.

Try This!
Complete activities and hands-on experiments.

Quizzes
Test your knowledge.

Slide Show
View images and captions, and prepare a presentation.

AV² was built to bridge the gap between print and digital. We encourage you to tell us what you like and what you want to see in the future.

Sign up to be an AV² Ambassador at www.av2books.com/ambassador.

Due to the dynamic nature of the Internet, some of the URLs and activities provided as part of AV² by Weigl may have changed or ceased to exist. AV² by Weigl accepts no responsibility for any such changes. All media enhanced books are regularly monitored to update addresses and sites in a timely manner. Contact AV² by Weigl at 1-866-649-3445 or av2books@weigl.com with any questions, comments, or feedback.